The Grasshopper

Written by June Loves
Illustrated by Ian Forss

One sunny day,
a green grasshopper went out
into the long, cool grass.
He was looking for an adventure.

Hippity, hippity, hop!

"Watch out for birds that swoop,"
said his mother.

 3

"Look out for cows that munch,"
said his father.

"Be careful of children that catch,"
said his aunt.

"Good morning, girls and boys.
We found a grasshopper."

"Let's take a look at this grasshopper,"
said the teacher.

One sunny day,
a green grasshopper went out
into the long, cool grass.
He was looking for an adventure.

Hippity, hippity, hop!